DID YOU KNOW?

SPORTS

20 THINGS YOU DIDN'T KNOW ABOUT

AUTO RACING

I0808668

THEIA LAKE

PowerKiDS press

Published in 2026 by The Rosen Publishing Group, Inc.
2544 Clinton Street, Buffalo, NY 14224

Copyright © 2026 by The Rosen Publishing Group, Inc.

All rights reserved. No part of this book may be reproduced in any form without permission in writing from the publisher, except by a reviewer.

Portions of this work were originally authored by Ryan Nagelhout and published as *20 Fun Facts About Autho Racing*. All new material in this edition was authored by Theia Lake.

Editor: Greg Roza
Book Design: Tanya Dellaccio Keeney

Photo Credits: Cover KOTOIMAGES/Shutterstock.com; pp. 5, 27 Jay Hirano/Shutterstock.com; p. 7 piemags/DCM/Alamy Images; p. 10 Felix Mizioznikov/Shutterstock.com; pp. 11, 29 Jens Mommens/Shutterstock.com; pp. 9, 12, 13, 14, 18, 19 Grindstone Media/Shutterstock.com; p. 15 https://upload.wikimedia.org/wikipedia/commons/a/a0/Milwaukee-Mile_Aug2009_wall.jpg; p. 16 danieleorsi/Shutterstock.com; p. 20 https://upload.wikimedia.org/wikipedia/en/0/0a/Louise_Smith.png; p. 21 Oskar SCHULER/Shutterstock.com; p. 22 Steven Hodel/Shutterstock.com; p. 23 https://upload.wikimedia.org/wikipedia/commons/c/c2/MarioAndrettiAndJohnAndrettiMay2007.jpg; p. 24 Lucia L/Shutterstock.com; p. 25 Cornel Pop/Shutterstock.com; p. 26 CHEN WS/Shutterstock.com.

Some of the images in this book illustrate individuals who are models. The depictions do not imply actual situations or events.

Cataloging-in-Publication Data

Names: Lake, Theia.
Title: 20 things you didn't know about auto racing / Theia Lake.
Description: Buffalo, New York : PowerKids Press, 2026. | Series: Did you know? Sports | Includes glossary and index.
Identifiers: ISBN 9781499450262 (pbk.) | ISBN 9781499450279 (library bound) | ISBN 9781499450286 (ebook)
Subjects: LCSH: Automobile racing–Juvenile literature.
Classification: LCC GV1029.13 L35 2026 | DDC 796.72-dc23

Manufactured in the United States of America

CPSIA Compliance Information: Batch #CSPK26. For Further Information contact Rosen Publishing at 1-800-237-9932.

Find us on

CONTENTS

PUT THE PEDAL TO THE METAL

Auto racing has been around for almost as long as cars! Race cars may have changed a lot since then, but the joy of watching them drive by at top speeds is still the same.

There's more to auto racing than just circling a track! Racing teams work together to suit their car to different conditions. There are many **circuits** to race, each with different rules and challenges, or problems, to face. Auto racing is a sport and an art!

Today, Formula One (F1) racing is one of the fastest-growing sports in America!

HOW IT STARTED

DID YOU KNOW?

The United States' first auto race was won by a driver going about 7 miles (11.3 km) per hour!

The *Chicago Times-Herald* race took place on a cold Thanksgiving Day, 1895, in Chicago, Illinois. This was shortly after the world's first auto race in France. Six drivers set out on the 54.4-mile (87.5 km) course. The winner was J. Frank Duryea.

Frank and his brother Charles Duryea made the Duryea Wagon, which Frank drove in the *Chicago Times-Herald* race. It was the only gas-powered American car in the race. Two of the racers drove electric cars, which stopped working in the cold!

Charles (left) and Frank (right) Duryea are shown here with the Duryea Wagon.

HOW IT'S GOING

DID YOU KNOW?

Today, IndyCars drive at speeds of 236 miles (380 km) per hour or more!

IndyCars have reached some of the top speeds in auto races. Formula 1 cars are also super fast, hitting speeds of 231.4 miles (372.4 km) per hour.

Both IndyCars and Formula 1 cars have raced at the Circuit of the Americas, a track in Austin, Texas. Both kinds of cars are single seaters, which means they're made for just one person to ride in. The speeds they reach differ depending on the circuits they're racing.

Many people think of the Indy 500 race in Speedway, Indiana, as the fastest auto race in the United States.

TO THE TRACK

DID YOU KNOW?

Racetracks are different shapes.

A track's speed is partly based on its shape. Road and street racecourses have many right and left turns. The most common racetrack shape is oval with four left turns. Some tracks are triangle-shaped with three left turns. Tracks of different lengths and shapes pose different challenges, or problems, to drivers.

Even if they have the same shape, no two racetracks are exactly alike.

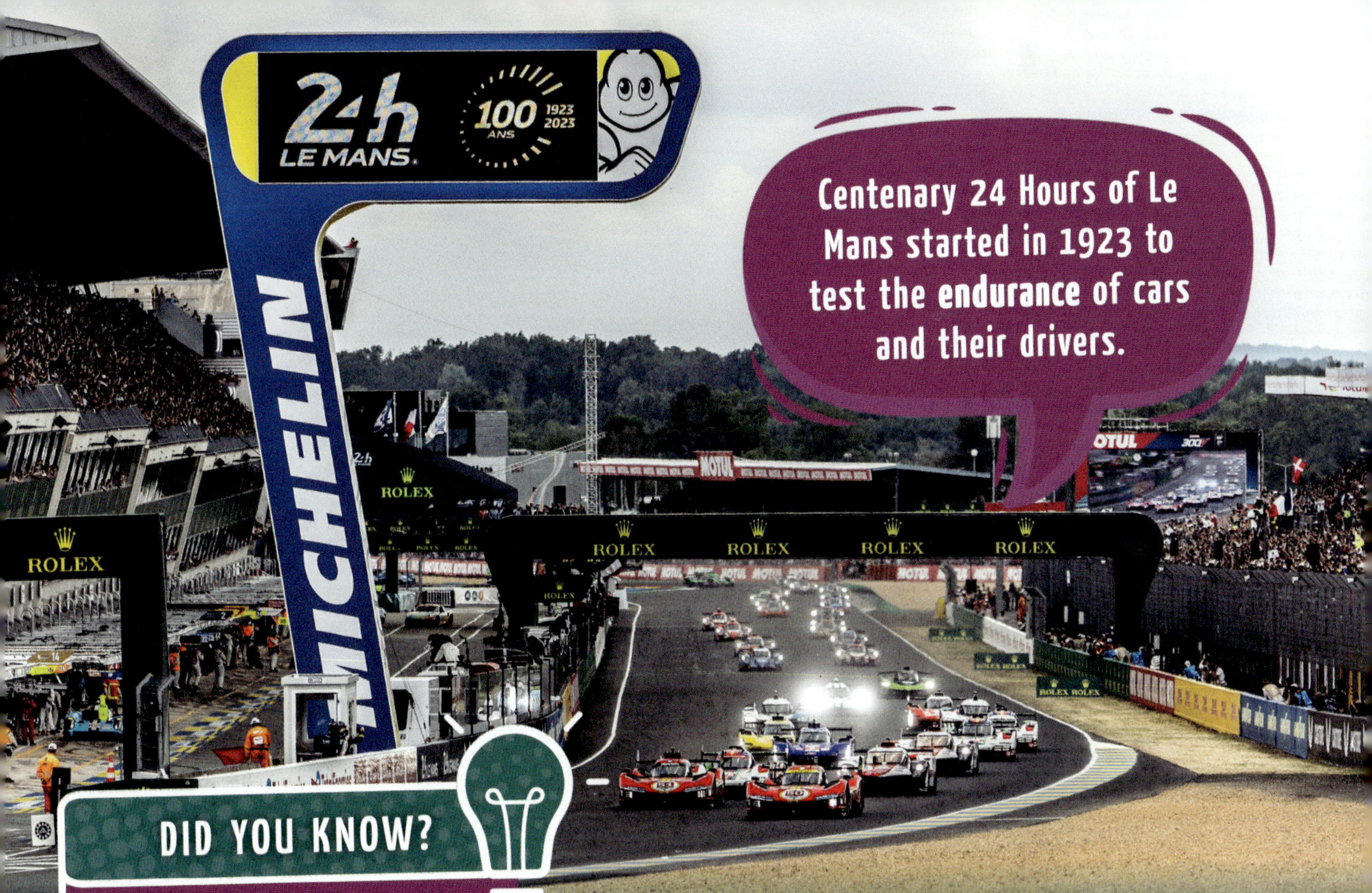

Centenary 24 Hours of Le Mans started in 1923 to test the **endurance** of cars and their drivers.

DID YOU KNOW?

Circuit de la Sarthe in Le Mans, France, is the biggest auto racetrack in the world.

The stands at Circuit de la Sarthe have a **capacity** of 263,500. Today, drivers race more than 2,796 miles (4,500 km) straight in the same car!

TOO FAST!

DID YOU KNOW?

NASCAR changed its rules to slow down cars for safety.

Drivers going superfast speeds led to dangerous **accidents** on NASCAR's Talladega and Daytona tracks. In April 2021, driver Joey Logano's car flew through the air and flipped onto its roof! But NASCAR slowed speeds at these tracks by 7 to 10 miles (11.3 to 16 km) per hour at these tracks to keep drivers safer.

Thankfully, Joey Logano wasn't hurt when his car flipped at the Talladega track.

Before restrictor plates were introduced, or first used, in 1988, accidents with cars going at speeds over 200 miles (321.9 km) per hour caused many people to get hurt.

DID YOU KNOW?

Restrictor plates are used to hold back engine power.

Restrictor plates restrict, or hold back, an engine's power. This forces a car to go slower. Restrictor plates make races safer and more **competitive**, too! That's because they cause different cars to have more comparable engine speeds.

SAFETY FIRST

DID YOU KNOW?

NASCAR race cars have metal pieces called flaps on the roof to keep them from going airborne, or flying into the air.

Hidden roof flaps are specially made to pop up when a car turns sideways. The flaps slow the flow of air over the car, pulling it back to the ground. These flaps are also supposed to keep the car from flipping over, but if a car's speed is too great, they won't work.

Roof flaps were introduced in 1994.

Using SAFER barriers (walls) may save drivers' lives!

DID YOU KNOW?

Today, race cars usually crash into SAFER walls!

SAFER stands for Steel and Foam Energy Reduction. SAFER walls are made of steel tubes and hard foam. This takes in the force of cars when they run into them! SAFER walls are softer than the concrete walls that were once used.

TALK ON THE TRACK

DID YOU KNOW?

Teams use radios to talk to drivers, but drivers can't talk to each other.

It's important for teams to be able to talk. How do they do this in the middle of a big, fast, noisy race? Race cars have special radios. A driver can tell their team if they're having trouble, and a team can tell their driver what to do.

Too much talk can make it hard for drivers to pay attention! Teams need to be careful about how and when they use their radios.

INDYCAR FLAGS

END OF THE RACE

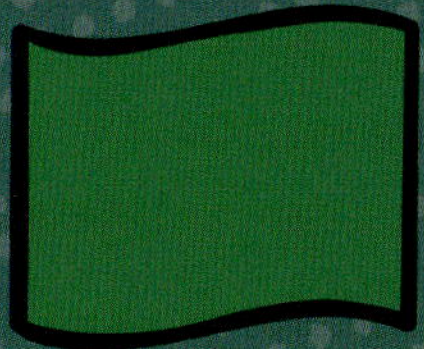

START OF THE RACE

TRACK IS SLIPPERY

CAUTION FLAG – SIGNALS THAT CARS MUST SLOW DOWN

A FASTER CAR IS APPROACHING

ONE LAP REMAINING

DRIVER MUST GO TO THE PIT TO SPEAK WITH OFFICIALS

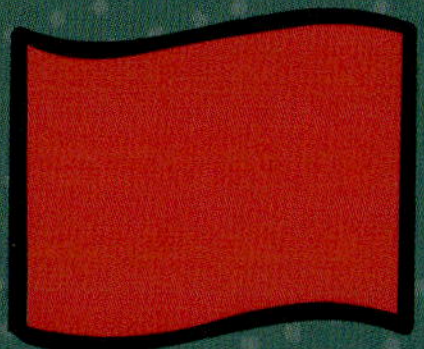

STOP

DRIVER IS DISQUALIFIED

DID YOU KNOW?

Racetracks use flags to talk to drivers!

A flag waver sits high above the start/finish line and lets drivers know what's happening in the race. Different flags signal different messages to drivers.

CARS, CARS, CARS!

DID YOU KNOW?

NASCAR drivers used to race regular cars.

NASCAR stands for National Association for Stock Car Racing. When NASCAR first started, drivers raced cars that were exactly like cars made in factories. "Stock" meant they couldn't be changed.

Today, stock cars are named after everyday cars, but really, they're specially built for extra speed and power.

DID YOU KNOW?

IndyCars have a push-to-pass button!

IndyCar drivers can use the push-to-pass button 10 times during a race.

IndyCars have a special button. It gives drivers a short boost of power from their engine. Based on the track where the cars are racing, the speed boost usually lasts 20 seconds. The boost makes it easier to pass cars at high speeds.

WOMEN IN MOTORSPORTS

DID YOU KNOW?

Stock car racer Louise Smith (1916–2006) was known as the First Lady of Racing.

Louise Smith helped lead the way for women in auto racing. She started racing in 1947 and quickly became known for her bravery and speed. She won 38 races in four **divisions** before she **retired** in 1956. The character named Barnstormer in the movie *Cars 3* is based on her!

Louise Smith was the first woman ever inducted, or brought into, the International Motorsports Hall of Fame.

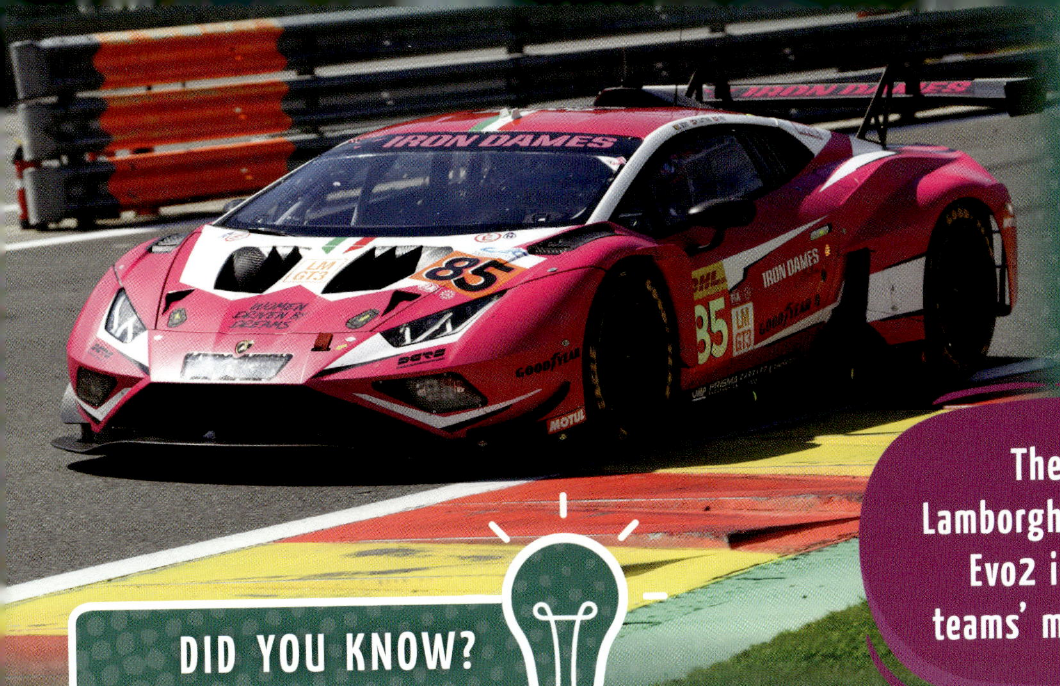

The Iron Dames' Lamborghini Huracán LMGT3 Evo2 is pink, like the teams' matching uniforms.

DID YOU KNOW?

The Iron Dames (which means "ladies") is the first all-female team in the history of endurance racing!

Founded in 2018, the Iron Dames is made up of four drivers: Rahel Frey, Michelle Gatting, Sarah Bovy, and Doriane Pin. They've taken part in competitions around the world, including the World Endurance Championship (WEC), and in the United States as part of the International Motor Sports Association (IMSA) series.

RECORD-MAKERS

DID YOU KNOW?

Mario Andretti is one of the greatest race car drivers of all time.

Italian American driver Mario Andretti is very well known. It's said that he can drive any kind of car in any kind of race. And he has! Andretti is the only driver ever to win the Indianapolis 500, the Daytona 500, and the Formula One World Championship.

Andretti is also the only driver to have won a race in the NASCAR Sprint Cup Series, Formula One, and an Indianapolis 500.

John Andretti founded the "Race for Riley," an annual go-kart race that rasies money for Riley Children's Hospital in Indianapolis, Indiana.

DID YOU KNOW?

Mario Andretti's nephew, John Andretti, was the first driver to do Double Duty.

Doing Double Duty means driving both the Indianapolis 500 and the NASCAR Coca-Cola 600 on the same day! In 1994, John Andretti finished 10th at the Indy 500. He then got on a plane to Charlotte, North Carolina, and drove the Coca-Cola 600!

FORCES OF POWER

DID YOU KNOW?

Horsepower has been used to measure engine power since before cars were invented!

One horsepower is the power needed to lift 33,000 pounds (14,968.5 kg) 1 foot (0.3 m) off the ground in 1 minute. Horsepower was first used by Scottish inventor James Watt during the 1700s. Today, the most powerful engines have more than 2,000 horsepower.

Dray horses, like the one pictured here, were used to measure horsepower.

You may have felt g-force while riding a roller coaster. Some coasters experience up to 5 Gs!

DID YOU KNOW?

F1 drivers can feel up to 5 Gs of power during a race!

When a car turns, brakes, or accelerates (speeds up), the driver feels a force similar to **gravity** called g-force. One g-force (1 G) is the same as the feel of gravity. Experiencing 2 Gs is like feeling twice as heavy, and so on.

ENGINES ROARING!

DID YOU KNOW?

An F1 race car's engine is dangerously noisy!

F1 engines make a noisy sound that can reach 140 **decibels**! That's as loud as a gunshot or a jet plane taking off! The Guinness World Records says that an F1 cockpit is the noisiest workplace in the world.

Noises over 120 decibels harm people's ears. It's important to wear headphones at an F1 race.

A race car workshop can also be a noisy place to work.

DID YOU KNOW?

Today, many F1 engines have been changed to be a little quieter (around 134 decibels).

F1 engines are super noisy because they're super powerful. They can go from 0 to 60 miles (96.6 km) per hour in 2.6 seconds! Today's F1 car engines have about 1,050 horsepower.

FULL SPEED AHEAD

Auto racing has changed a lot over the past 100 years. As **technology** advanced, or moved forward, race cars became faster and more powerful. Technology has also helped make racetracks, cars, and drivers safer from deadly crashes.

Today, car technology continues to **evolve**. In 2014, an all-electric racing division called Formula E hit the track. More women are taking part in auto racing, breaking down barriers in the historically male sport. As drivers race toward the future at full speed, what other changes will they see coming down the road?

Still want to learn more fun facts about auto racing? Then check out the books and websites on page 31!

GLOSSARY

accident: A sudden event resulting in loss or injury.

capacity: The amount of people that can fit into a place.

caution: Care taken to avoid mistakes or accidents.

circuit: A chain of racetracks all running the same type of events. Also, the entire slate of races of one type for a full season.

competitive: Having a strong desire to win or be the best at something.

decibel: A unit for measuring the relative loudness of sounds.

division: The branch of a sport.

endurance: The ability to last a long time under pressure.

evolve: To grow and change over time.

gravity: The force that pulls objects toward Earth's center.

retire: To stop doing a certain job.

technology: A method that uses science to solve problems and the tools used to solve those problems.

FOR MORE INFORMATION

BOOKS

Colson, Rob. *Racecars.* New York, NY: Crabtree Publishing Company, 2022.

Rule, Heather. *GOATs of Auto Racing*. Minneapolis, MN: SportsZone, 2022.

WEBSITES

Formula 1

www.formula1.com/en/latest

Learn more about Formula 1 racing.

NASCAR Kids

www.nascarkids.com

Play fun games, read about drivers, and find out more about the world of NASCAR!

Publisher's note to educators and parents: Our editors have carefully reviewed these websites to ensure that they are suitable for students. Many websites change frequently, however, and we cannot guarantee that a site's future contents will continue to meet our high standards of quality and educational value. Be advised that students should be closely supervised whenever they access the internet.

INDEX